BECOMING A WOMAN OF *purpose*

CYNTHIA HEALD

BECOMING A WOMAN OF purpose

NAVPRESS®

BRINGING TRUTH TO LIFE

OUR GUARANTEE TO YOU

We believe so strongly in the message of our books that we are making this quality guarantee to you. If for any reason you are disappointed with the content of this book, return the title page to us with your name and address and we will refund to you the list price of the book. To help us serve you better, please briefly describe why you were disappointed. Mail your refund request to: NavPress, P.O. Box 35002, Colorado Springs, CO 80935.

The Navigators is an international Christian organization. Our mission is to advance the gospel of Jesus and His kingdom into the nations through spiritual generations of laborers living and discipling among the lost. We see a vital movement of the gospel, fueled by prevailing prayer, flowing freely through relational networks and out into the nations where workers for the kingdom are next door to everywhere.

NavPress is the publishing ministry of The Navigators. The mission of NavPress is to reach, disciple, and equip people to know Christ and make Him known by publishing life-related materials that are biblically rooted and culturally relevant. Our vision is to stimulate spiritual transformation through every product we publish.

ISBN-13: 978-1-57683-831-0
ISBN-10: 1-57683-831-5

Cover design by Disciple Design
Cover photo by Creatas
Creative Team: Steve Parolini, Darla Hightower, Arvid Wallen, Glynese Northam

Unless otherwise identified, all Scripture quotations in this publication are taken from the *New American Standard Bible* (NASB), © The Lockman Foundation 1960, 1962, 1963, 1968, 1971, 1972, 1973, 1975, 1977. Other versions used include: the *HOLY BIBLE: NEW INTERNATIONAL VERSION*® (NIV®), Copyright ©1973, 1978, 1984 by International Bible Society, used by permission of Zondervan Publishing House, all rights reserved; *The New Testament in Modern English* (PH), J. B. Phillips Translator, © J.B. Phillips 1958, 1960, 1972, used by permission of Macmillan Publishing Company; *The New English Bible* (NEB), © 1961, 1970, The Delegates of the Oxford University Press and The Syndics of the Cambridge University Press; and the *King James Version* (KJV).

Heald, Cynthia.
    Becoming a woman of purpose : a bible study / by Cynthia Heald. A bible study on becoming a woman of purpose 105 p. ; 22 cm.
    Includes bibliographical references (p. 97-101).
    ISBN 1-57683-831-5
    1. Bible—Study and teaching. 2. Woman (Christian theology)—Biblical teaching. 3. Christian life.
248.843 H434bp

Printed in the United States of America

4 5 6 7 8 / 10 09 08

Contents

Suggestions for Using This Study

This study is designed for both individual as well as small group use, and for women of any age or family status.

Many of the questions will guide you into Scripture passages. Ask God to reveal His truth to you through His Word, and don't be concerned about "wrong" answers. Bible study references—such as commentaries, encyclopedias, and handbooks—can help you understand particular passages by providing historical background, contexts, and common interpretations. (In a few cases, you'll need access to a standard dictionary—such as *Webster's, Random House,* or the *Oxford American*—for general word definitions.)

Other questions will ask you to reflect on your own life. Approach these questions honestly and thoughtfully; however, if you're doing this study in a group, don't feel that you must reveal private details of your life experiences. Use the questions for "Contemplation and Prayer" at the close of each chapter to help you work through significant issues raised by your study. If you keep a personal journal, you might want to write these reflections there rather than in this guide.

You might want to memorize the key Scripture reference for each chapter, which is the Scripture used for "Contemplation and Prayer." You'll find that memorizing God's Word will enrich your study and deepen the significance and impact of your personal reflection.

The quotes from classic thinkers and writers have been carefully selected to enhance your understanding and enjoyment of the content in *Becoming a Woman of Purpose*. The references for these quotations (see the "Notes" section at the back of the book) will also furnish an excellent reading list for your own devotional reading and study.

PREFACE

All of us have been encouraged at some time or another to determine what our purpose is in doing a project, planning an event, or setting life goals.

I used to think that trying to decide on a purpose was a waste of time. My philosophy was, "If something needs doing, just do it! Why spend the time and energy trying to decide why it should get done?" But I have lived long enough to experience disillusionment when, after working hard on a project, it seemed to yield minimal results. I have since realized that having a purpose frees me from focusing on results. Instead, I am able to rest in the accomplishment of an underlying purpose that is not dependent on circumstances.

And so it is with God's work in our lives. If we can begin to understand His purpose, what He is about in our world and in our lives, then our perspective on what happens day to day takes on new meaning.

If I am God's child, what is His purpose for me? What does He want to accomplish? What is important to Him? These are valid questions that need to be answered if we are to experience genuine fulfillment and joy in life.

This is not a study that centers on discovering your own individualized purpose in life. Nor is it an exhaustive treatment of this subject. However, it is my hope that this study will be a catalyst for you to understand God and His purposes in a fresh way. For it is in comprehending the purposes of God that you will find the true, eternal purpose for your life.

May God richly bless you as you become a woman of purpose for His glory.

CHAPTER ONE

God's purpose:
A People Who Will Reflect His Glory

❦

You are worthy, our Lord and God, to receive glory and honor and power, for you created all things, and by your will they were created and have their being.

REVELATION 4:11, NIV

The proper understanding of everything in life begins with God. No one will ever understand the necessity of conversion who does not know why God created us. He created us "in his image" so that we would image forth his glory in the world. We were made to be prisms refracting the light of God's glory into all of life. Why God should want to give us a share in shining with his glory is a great mystery. Call it grace or mercy or love—it is an unspeakable wonder. Once we were not. Then we existed for the glory of God![1]

JOHN PIPER, *DESIRING GOD*

11

I once saw a cartoon of a man who walks up to an information booth and asks the person behind the counter, "Who am I?" and "What am I doing here?" Good questions! Why have we been created? What is God's purpose for us? What prompted God to "make man in our image, in our likeness"? To begin to comprehend God's purpose helps to establish a foundation for us to embrace life and to honor the Lord. Certainly everything in life begins with God and He alone is worthy to receive the glory due His name. What is amazing is that God desires relationship with us and wants us to reflect His glory!

God's Purpose: To Receive Glory

The Hebrew word translated "glory" comes from a root that means "heavy" or "weighty." The word is normally used in figurative sense to suggest an impressive or worthy person. . . . But the glory of God is objective. It is rooted not in the evaluation of others, but in his very nature. When God's glory is unveiled and recognized, all those things in which human beings take pride fade to nothingness.[2]

Lawrence O. Richards

1. What do these Scriptures tell us about God's glory?

    Psalm 19:1

    Psalm 115:1

Isaiah 6:3

1 Corinthians 10:31

___

2. a. God's glory is all around us! In what ways have you seen God's glory displayed in creation?

   b. What was your response?

For God's ultimate objective, as the Bible declares it, is threefold — to vindicate His rule and righteousness by showing His sovereignty in judgment upon sin; to ransom and redeem His chosen people; and to be loved and praised by them for His glorious acts of love and self-vindication. God seeks what we should seek — His glory, in and through men — and it is for the securing of this end, ultimately, that He is jealous.[3]

J. I. Packer

God's Purpose: To Have a People for His Own

3. David proclaimed, "Your eyes have seen my unformed substance; and in Your book were all written the days that were ordained for me, when as yet there was not one of them" (Psalm 139:16).

God has made it very clear in His Word that we have been created thoughtfully and purposefully. Why did God take the dust of the ground and breathe the breath of life into Adam? Read these verses and record your answers.

Psalm 149:4

2 Thessalonians 2:13-14

Titus 2:11-14

4. God has redeemed a people for His own. Write down your thoughts concerning God's desire to be in relationship with you.

What is man's purpose here? According to the text, creation exists for man. But since God made man like himself, man's dominion over the world and his filling the world is a display—and imaging forth—of God. God's aim, therefore, was that man would so act that he mirror forth God, who has ultimate dominion. Man is given the exalted status of image-bearer not so he would become arrogant and autonomous (as he tried to do in the fall), but so he would reflect the glory of his Maker whose image he bears. God's purpose in creation, therefore, was to fill the earth with his own glory.[4]

John Piper

AUTHOR'S REFLECTION—In considering the magnificence of God and His great desire for His own to honor Him, I have been struck with my lack of even thinking about or acknowledging God's glory on a daily basis. My tendency is to view God as mainly Someone who helps, comforts, and guides, which He does, but my worship and adoration of Him is sporadic and shallow in comparison to who He really is. I want to begin to set aside special times just to focus on God, and God alone. I want to read and memorize Scripture that proclaims and guides me in praising Him for His majestic glory. I want to prepare myself for the eternal worship I will be giving our Lord. I realize that I am missing a vital part of my relationship with God by not consistently acknowledging His preeminence.

I have also been struck with the apostle Paul's exhortation that everything we do should be done to bring glory to God. Does God really mean *everything*? When I seriously consider this admonition, it has a profound effect on my choices and my way of life! If I read this book, will God be pleased? If I do this activity, will it cause others to want to praise God? If I listen to this music, will it enable me to worship God? If I say these words, will it bring glory to God? If my purpose is to reflect the majesty of God, then all of my decisions are based on "Will God receive glory?"

All Your works shall give thanks to You, O LORD,
And Your godly ones shall bless You.
They shall speak of the glory of Your kingdom,
And talk of Your power;
To make known to the sons of men Your mighty acts
And the glory of the majesty of Your kingdom.

Psalm 145:10-12

How I need to give thanks to God for His creation, for His mighty acts. How I need to bless God by speaking of His power and kingdom. How I need to order my life around one incredible thought: *God is to be honored in all I do.*

My heart's desire is to be so overwhelmed with our incomparable, awesome God that my life cannot help but bring Him glory.

A. W. Tozer comments on God's covenant with Abraham in Genesis 17:

> Abraham, I am trying to tell you something—something very important. I want you to listen and to comprehend. Abraham, you were made in My image and you were designed for a single purpose: to worship and glorify Me. . . . If you do not honor this purpose, your life will degenerate into shallow, selfish, humanistic pursuits . . . commit your whole life and future into My hands. Let Me as your Creator and God fulfill in you My perfect design. It is My great desire that you become a faithful and delighted worshiper at My throne. . . . When you have found Me, your Creator, your Redeemer and your Lord, you have found everything you need! It will be your privilege to trust and obey. It will be My privilege to bless you, guide you and sustain you.[5]

God's Purpose for Me (For Contemplation and Prayer)

5. Over the next few days think about God's glory and His desire for you to reflect His glory. To help your reflection and application, carefully read and consider the following verse.

> 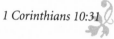Because, whatever you do, eating or drinking or anything else, everything should be done to bring glory to God.
>
> *1 Corinthians 10:31*

Use the following questions to guide your meditation.

6. What in my life does not bring God glory?

7. How can I become more aware of choosing to honor God in all I do?

SUGGESTED SCRIPTURE MEMORY: 1 Corinthians 10:31

CHAPTER TWO

God's purpose:
TO CONFORM US TO CHRIST

❧

The secret is simply this: Christ in you! Yes, Christ in you bringing with him the hope of all the glorious things to come.

COLOSSIANS 1:27, PH

So I saw with no less clearness, that the essence of religion consisted in the soul's conformity to God, and acting above all selfish views, for His glory, longing to be for Him, to live to Him, and please and honor Him in all things.[1]

DAVID BRAINERD

The Word became flesh, and dwelt among us, and we saw His glory, glory as of the only begotten from the Father, full of grace and truth" (John 1:14). In the fullness of time, God sent His Son to show us His glory and to purchase our redemption. God's heart, as our Father, is for us to come to Him through our acceptance of Jesus Christ as His Son and His death on the cross as purification of our sins. When we believe in Jesus Christ, we become new creations and Christ begins to live within us. Only as we are in Christ, can we hope to be what God intends. His purpose becomes real and transforming as we yield to the process He chooses for us to replicate His character. At great price God purchased our salvation and He continues His sanctifying work in us so that we will be transformed into His image and thereby glorify Him.

God's Purpose: To Bring Us to Himself

1. God desires for us to come to Him and to know Him. He loves us and has fully provided for our union with Him. What do the following Scriptures reveal about how God has made it possible for us to be in relationship with Him?

   John 5:24

   Colossians 2:9-10

   1 Timothy 2:3-6

2. What is your understanding of what it means to have a personal relationship with Jesus Christ?

The Lord Jesus Christ was eternally rich, glorious and exalted; but "though He was rich, yet for your sakes He became poor." . . . Poverty must be enriched by Him in whom are infinite treasures before it can venture to commune; and guilt must lose itself in imputed and imparted righteousness ere the soul can walk in fellowship with purity. Jesus must clothe His people in His own garments, or He cannot admit them into His palace of glory; and He must wash them in His own blood, or else they will be too defiled for the embrace of His fellowship. O believer, herein is love! For your sake the Lord Jesus "became poor" that He might lift you up into communion with Himself.[2]

Charles H. Spurgeon

God's Purpose: To Make Us Like Himself

3. Once we have accepted Jesus Christ as our Savior and Lord, God's Spirit immediately begins to live within us. He also begins to work in our lives, for He has a plan for us. Read the following verses and write down God's purposes.

Romans 8:29

Ephesians 4:22-24

1 Thessalonians 4:3-7

4. What are your thoughts about what it means to be conformed to the image of Christ? (You might want to look up the word *conform* in a dictionary.)

> The one marvellous secret of a holy life lies not in imitating Jesus, but in letting the perfections of Jesus manifest themselves in my mortal flesh. Sanctification is "Christ in you." It is His wonderful life that is imparted by faith as a sovereign gift of God's grace.[3]
>
> *Oswald Chambers*

5. God takes responsibility for our growth and sanctification. What can you learn about God's commitment to us from these Scriptures?

Ephesians 2:10

Philippians 1:3-6

Philippians 2:12-13

6. How does knowing God's commitment to complete His work encourage you in your life of faith?

The spiritual life does not consist in the withdrawal of self, of initiative, or of the consciousness of responsibility. . . . Thus it is seen that the actual experience into which the believer is brought as a result of dependence upon the Holy Spirit is not a coercion of his will, but a larger and more effective exercise of it. It is not a matter of the Holy Spirit compelling the one whom He empowers to make a choice of right ideals whether that one wills to do so or not; it is the deeper, more effective, and more normal achievement by the Spirit of inclining the one who depends upon Him to *will* in the sense of desire, and to *do* in the sense of complete accomplishment of that which constitutes the will of God.[4]

Lewis Sperry Chafer

AUTHOR'S REFLECTION—As a young teenager I accepted Christ as my personal Savior. I vividly remember our pastor asking me, "Do you believe that Jesus Christ is the Son of God and that He died for your sins?" That night I was baptized and ever since I have sensed the Lord's presence in my life.

It wasn't until I was an adult, though, that I began to understand that God wanted to conform me to the image of His Son. One of His major ways of sanctifying me was giving me three children in three years. Two of them were eleven months apart, and I'm not a real baby person! I think that God looked at me and said, "If I am ever going to begin to get any fruit of the Spirit into this woman, she needs to have all these children at once!" What better way for me to learn patience, self-control, gentleness, kindness, love, joy, faithfulness, and goodness. (Notice I didn't mention peace.) It was in the midst of these child-raising years that I realized my great need to fully surrender my life to God and allow Him to begin to transform my life according to His plan.

This is what God is after—as our Father, He wants us to have a strong family resemblance to Him. He uses all sorts of ways to mold us and to bring us to dependence upon Him. For some, this sanctifying process may involve not having children, not being married. For others it is marriage, children, parents, and jobs that God will use to conform us to the image of Christ.

God has purchased us by the blood of His Son and as a faithful Father, He desires for us to grow in Christlikeness, which is the very best and the highest good for any of us.

> There is always a tremendous battle before sanctification is realized—something within us pushing with resentment against the demands of Christ. . . . In the process of sanctification, the Spirit of God will strip me down until there is nothing left but myself, and that is the place of death. . . . Am I willing and determined to hand over my simple naked self to God? Once I am, He will immediately sanctify me completely, and my life will be free from being determined and persistent toward anything except God.[5]
>
> *Oswald Chambers*

God's Purpose for Me (For Contemplation and Prayer)

7. Over the next few days, think about God's desire to bring you to Himself and to work in you so that you can grow into the likeness of Christ. To help your reflection and application, carefully consider the following verse.

> All of us who are Christians have no veils on our faces, but reflect like mirrors the glory of the Lord. We are transfigured by the Spirit of the Lord in ever-increasing splendour into his own image.
>
> *2 Corinthians 3:18,* PH

Use the following questions to guide your meditation.

8. How might I be hindering God's desire to make me like His Son?

9. In what way am I a "mirror" for the Lord?

SUGGESTED SCRIPTURE MEMORY: 2 Corinthians 3:18

CHAPTER THREE

God's purpose:
To Love His People

How great is the love the Father has lavished on us, that we should be called children of God! And that is what we are!

1 JOHN 3:1, NIV

In God there is no hunger that needs to be filled, only plenteousness that desires to give. . . . God, who needs nothing, loves into existence wholly superfluous creatures in order that he may love and perfect them.[1]

C. S. LEWIS, *THE FOUR LOVES*

God, in all His glory and majesty, desires for us to know Him fully and to impart Himself to us. God longs to love us for He knows that His love is the only love that frees and completes us. His love is the only love that will truly satisfy us, for it is eternal and unconditional. God, through history, has communicated His love and desire for a people called by His Name. In order for us to want to reflect God's glory, we must comprehend God's great love for us. David knew of God's love for him, for he sang, "For Your lovingkindness toward me is great" (Psalm 86:13).

God's Purpose: To Love Us

In John 15, Jesus says, "Just as the Father has loved Me, I have also loved you; abide in My love" (verse 9). God desperately wants us to receive His love—even bask in it! But God will not force us to love Him; He initiates and He waits. Jesus gives us a beautiful example of God's love in Luke 15:11-32.

1. How is God's love revealed in the father's response to the return of the younger son (verses 20-24)?

2. How does the father's response to the complaint of the elder son reveal God's love (verses 25-32)?

3. What does this story tell you about God's love?

It is wrong to speak of God's need of love from his creation, but remember how God himself expressed his longing for that love: like a father starved for some response, *any* response, from his rebellious children; like a jilted lover who, against all reason, gives his faithless beloved one more chance. Those are the images God summoned up again and again throughout the time of the prophets. The deepest longings we feel on earth, as parents, as lovers, are mere flickers of the hungering desire God feels for us. It is a desire that cost him the Incarnation and the Crucifixion.[2]

Philip Yancey

God's Purpose: To Be Loved

4. Throughout history God has proved and communicated His love for His people. We talk about God's love for us, but rarely do we consider God's heart to be loved in return. Luke 13:34 gives us a glimpse of God's earnest desire for our love. What does the imagery Jesus uses convey about His longing to be loved?

That wail of grief over Jerusalem has about it a quality almost like shyness. Jesus, who could destroy Jerusalem with a word, who could call down legions of angels to force subjection, instead looks over the city and weeps. God holds back; he hides himself; he weeps. Why?

Because he desires what power can never win. He is
a king who wants not subservience, but love. Thus,
rather than mowing down Jerusalem, Rome, and every
other worldly power, he chose the slow, hard way of
Incarnation, love, and death. A conquest from within.[3]

Philip Yancey

---

5. Hosea 11:1-4 pictures God's love for His people, Israel. What do you
notice in this passage about God's tenderness toward those He loves?

What does God get in return? He gets adopted children
who are petty, petulant, spoiled, demanding, argumen-
tative, mistrusting, angry, critical, and an irritant to
everyone but God. . . . Nevertheless, our God bought us
with an infinite price and intends on seeing us crowned
with His very glory. Is it any wonder that Paul shouts at
the top of his lungs, "I pray that you, being rooted and
established in love, may have power, together with all the
saints, to grasp how wide and long and high and deep is
the love of Christ, and to know this love that surpasses
knowledge—that you may be filled to the measure of
all the fullness of God" (Ephesians 3:17-19). Paul prays
that I will know the unknowable love and be so full of
God that I achieve dimensions of being that reflect the
boundlessness of God.[4]

Dan B. Allender

6. What is your response to God's desire to love you?

AUTHOR'S REFLECTION—I am overwhelmed with God's steadfast love for His people. His love is freely given, is unconditional, is undeserved, and cannot be earned. Nothing has been too costly for God to express His love. The ultimate confirmation of His desire is His sending His Son to die for us. Someone has said that the Cross is God shouting through history how much He loves.

The very best thing I can do for myself is to seek to grasp the depth of God's love for me. If I am secure in God's devotion, then I am free to love others without depending on them to meet my need for love. Only God's love is everlasting, unreserved, and complete. His love forgives, molds, disciplines, and equips me to live. There is no equal or substitute for God's love. Psalm 16:4 warns us, "The sorrows of those who have bartered for another god will be multiplied." Whereas those who receive the Lord's love have their treasuries filled with the best that God has to offer.

Why would I want anything else, but the precious love of God?

> In the Incarnation and Crucifixion, Christ is the ultimate expression of God's love. Looking at the Cross, we too can be sure that this God of love will, "along with [Christ], graciously give us all things" (Romans 8:32). Convinced that nothing "will be able to separate us from the love of God that is in Christ Jesus our Lord" (Romans 8:39), we face life and death with confidence. In Christ every event in our personal history takes on fresh perspective, for the Cross assures us of God's endless love.[5]
>
> *Lawrence O. Richards*

God's Purpose for Me (For Contemplation and Prayer)

7. Over the next few days, think about God's love for you and His desire for you to return His love. To help your reflection and application, carefully consider the verse given below.

> Therefore the LORD longs to be gracious to you,
> And therefore He waits on high to have compassion
>   on you.
> For the LORD is a God of justice;
> How blessed are all those who long for Him.
>
> *Isaiah 30:18*

Use these questions to guide your meditation.

8. What barriers in my life keep me from receiving God's love?

9. How am I blessed by His love?

SUGGESTED SCRIPTURE MEMORY: Isaiah 30:18

CHAPTER FOUR

God's purpose:
To Establish His Kingdom

❧

"Remember the former things long past,
For I am God, and there is no other;
I am God, and there is no one like Me,
Declaring the end from the beginning,
And from ancient times things which have not been
    done,
Saying, 'My purpose will be established,
And I will accomplish all My good pleasure.'"

ISAIAH 46:9-10

*Toward all this God is moving with infinite wisdom
and perfect precision of action. No one can dissuade
Him from His purposes; nothing turn Him aside from
His plans. Since He is omniscient, there can be no
unforeseen circumstance, no accidents. As He is sovereign, there can be no countermanded orders, no break-
down in authority; and as He is omnipotent, there can
be no want of power to achieve His chosen ends. God
is sufficient unto Himself for all these things.*[1]

A. W. TOZER, *THE KNOWLEDGE OF THE HOLY*

*G*od declares, "I am He, I am the first, I am also the last" (Isaiah 48:12). Certainly God is the beginning and the end! He created the universe and it is His. The Lord's grand design for everyone is right on schedule and His plan and purpose will be fulfilled. Job humbly acknowledged God's sovereignty: "I know that You can do all things, and that no purpose of Yours can be thwarted" (Job 42:2). How encouraging to know that this life ultimately is part of God's accomplishing His eternal good pleasure. God superintends His world and He knows exactly what is going on with each of us. It's important that we begin to understand God's sovereign rule in our lives because once we do, we will have hope, security, and a desire to persevere. Jonathan Edwards wrote, "Absolute sovereignty is what I love to ascribe to God."[2]

God's Purpose: To Establish His Sovereignty

1. A king has supreme authority and we are told that "God is the King of all the earth" (Psalm 47:7). Read Isaiah 40:1-31 and write down the descriptive phrases and images that convey God's sovereignty.

2. The Everlasting God has no equal! What one thought on the sovereignty of God encourages you in your relationship with Him?

The God of the Bible is not weak; He is strong. He is all-mighty. Nothing happens without His permission or apart from His purposes—even evil. Nothing disturbs or puzzles Him. His purposes are always accomplished. Therefore those who know Him rightly act with boldness, assured that God is with them to accomplish His own desirable purposes in their lives.[3]

James Boice

God's Purpose: To Establish His Kingdom

3. If God is truly sovereign and no purpose of His can be thwarted, then some hard questions emerge. Why is the world like it is today? Why is there sin and suffering? Although we can't fully answer these questions, we can gain insights from Jesus' parable of the wheat and the weeds (Matthew 13:24-30,36-43). Record your observations concerning God's sovereignty over evil in establishing His kingdom.

The power of Satan and his fallen angels is limited. They are but finite creatures who can do nothing outside the permissive will of God. Satan could do nothing against Job (and this was his complaint) until divinely permitted to do so. Satan and his angels are in possession of great knowledge, but they are not omniscient; they have vast power, when permitted to employ it, but they are not omnipotent; they cover the world by their delegated responsibility, but they are not omnipresent. They can suggest evil, but cannot coerce the will of another creature. They may spread snares and devices to ruin the children of God, but they cannot compel any other being to comply with their designs. They have power over nature when permitted to use it, but they can create nothing, nor can they employ God's creation other than as He decrees. They never defeated God. In truth, God uses Satan as an instrument to chasten and correct the erring saints. The knowledge of these limitations cannot but be a comfort to those Christians who take seriously their conflict with the powers of darkness.[4]

Lewis Sperry Chafer

---

4. A king is not a king without a kingdom, and so it is with God. Despite the activity of Satan, and God's extraordinary patience, His kingdom is being established (for the present, it is within us) and will be victorious. What specific assurances concerning the certainty of God's kingdom can you find in the following passages?

Psalm 9

Zephaniah 3:8-9

5. In today's difficult world, what comfort can you receive from the assurance of God's sovereignty?

In my own times of disappointment with God, I have called on him to act with power. I have prayed against political tyranny and unfairness and injustice. I have prayed for a miracle, for proof of God's existence. But as I read the prophets' descriptions of the day when God finally will take off all the wraps, one prayer overwhelms all others: "God, I hope I'm not around then." God freely admits he is holding back his power, but he restrains himself for our benefit. For all scoffers who call for direct action from the heavens, the prophets have ominous advice: Just wait.[5]

Philip Yancey

AUTHOR'S REFLECTION — I agree with Jonathan Edwards — absolute sovereignty is what I love about God. Just to know that the Lord is never caught off guard or surprised by anything that happens gives me great comfort. To be reminded that Satan is a defeated foe and that the lawlessness around us will be righteously judged enables me to endure while "looking for the blessed hope and the appearing of the glory of our great God and Savior, Christ Jesus" (Titus 2:13).

To be loved by God and to be a part of His powerful kingdom is an incredible privilege. Not to trust God with my life or to doubt His wisdom in the affairs of this world is to presume that He is not truly the almighty God. In a sense, I have a choice of living as a secure, beloved child of the King, or living as an anxious, frustrated child whose God is not all-powerful or compassionate.

When tragic, unexplainable situations enter my life, I must be willing to wrestle with my Sovereign, to honestly come to Him with my broken heart. I must also be willing to rest in His wise ability to accomplish His purpose in His way for His kingdom and for me.

I know *I* cannot rule my life and find true fulfillment. I praise God for His desire to "take me under His wing" and to be Lord of my life. I love Him for His sovereignty!

> When I say God is in control, I do not mean that God is controlling everything that is happening. If God were actually controlling, there would be no sin. But God is in control, meaning He allows people to do what they want; and sometimes He intervenes, sometimes He stops them.
>
> God is in control in the sense that eventually everything is going to work out according to His plan. He is in control of the future. God is in control of the present in the sense that nothing happens that He does not permit to happen. God permits many things to happen that He does not will to happen. He does not want me to sin, but He does permit me to sin.[6]
>
> *C. Donald Cole*

God's Purpose for Me (For Contemplation and Prayer)

6. Over the next few days, think about God's sovereignty and what it means to be a citizen of His kingdom. To help your reflection and application from this session, carefully consider the following verses.

The counsel of the LORD stands forever,
The plans of His heart from generation to generation.
Blessed is the nation whose God is the LORD,
The people whom He has chosen for His own
    inheritance.

Psalm 33:11-12

Use the following questions to guide your meditation.

7. In what ways do I overlook God's sovereignty in my understanding of Him?

8. In what ways will my life be blessed as I trust in God's sovereign ability to accomplish His purpose in the world and in my own life?

SUGGESTED SCRIPTURE MEMORY: Psalm 33:11-12

CHAPTER FIVE

God's purpose:
TO ACCOMPLISH
HIS PLAN FOR GOOD

We know that God causes all things to work together for good to those who love God, to those who are called according to His purpose. For those whom He foreknew, He also predestined to become conformed to the image of His Son, so that He would be the first born among many brethren.

ROMANS 8:28-29

When once you are rightly related to God by salvation and sanctification, remember that wherever you are, you are put there by God; and by the reaction of your life on the circumstances around you, you will fulfil God's purpose, as long as you keep in the light as God is in the light.[1]

OSWALD CHAMBERS,
MY UTMOST FOR HIS HIGHEST

*T*he apostle Paul speaks with great confidence ("we *know*") concerning God's intention of working *all* things together for good for those called to His purpose. To begin to comprehend that God is at work weaving the events of our lives for our welfare is essential for my trust in Him. If I love God and have been called to His purpose, then I can be sure that He takes each circumstance of my life and causes it for good. David had been seized by the Philistines and this is his prayer: "You have taken account of my wanderings; Put my tears in Your bottle. Are they not in Your book? ... This I know, that God is for me" (Psalm 56:8-9). God knew exactly what was happening to David, and David knew that God was for him.

God's Purpose: To Call Us to His Plan

1. It is such an affirmation to be chosen by someone! It is important to understand God's commitment to us in order to trust Him to work for our good. Read Ephesians 1:3-14 and write down the decisive statements that communicate how God has chosen us.

2. Choose one statement or image from Ephesians 1:3-14 that is especially striking to you. What is your response to this blessing that God has given you?

While there is very much in the doctrine of divine elec-
tion which transcends the limitations of the finite understanding, it is true that man originates nothing — not
even sin, since sin began with the angels of God. It is
God who hath chosen His elect; and while this selection
is both sovereign and final, nevertheless not one human
being who desires to be saved and who complies with
the necessary terms of the gospel, will ever be lost.[2]

Lewis Sperry Chafer

God's Purpose: To Work for Good

God calls us, and He sovereignly begins to work all things for our good in
order that we might "become conformed to the image of His Son." The
Greek word for "good," *agathos,* "views the good as useful or profitable
and is the word chosen when moral goodness is being considered."[3]

---

3. Based on the following Scriptures, how do you think God defines
   good?

   Deuteronomy 10:12-13

   Matthew 5:1-12

4. Contrast God's idea of what is good with what people in our society today typically think is good for their lives.

5. What "good" do you want for your life?

> The teaching of Jesus is out of all proportion to our natural way of looking at things and it comes with astonishing discomfort to begin with. We have slowly to form our walk and conversation on the line of the precepts of Jesus Christ as the Holy Spirit applies them to our circumstances. The Sermon on the Mount is not a set of rules and regulations: it is a statement of the life we will live when the Holy Spirit is getting His way with us.[4]
>
> *Oswald Chambers*

6. We are told in Romans 8:28 that *all* things work together for good. But what does "all" really mean? Study these passages and write in the columns what God uses in our lives and how it works for good.

WHAT GOD USED	THE GOOD THAT RESULTED
Genesis 45:1-15; 50:16-21	
John 9:1-12,35-38	
2 Corinthians 12:7-10	

There is nothing inherently good about birth defects, natural calamities, and the host of other adversities we may encounter. And when evil is perpetrated against us by someone else, there certainly is no inherent good in it. But in God's infinite wisdom and love, He takes all the events of our lives—both good and bad—and blends them together so that they work together ultimately for our good, the good that He intends.[5]

Jerry Bridges

7. Does realizing God's faithfulness to work all things for good help you in trusting Him? Why, or why not?

> Lord do not stay Your hand; cut away until I am brought out into the fair lines and lineaments of the image of God. … But rest assured that if you love God all things will work together for your good. … To love God is the only true evidence of being His "called" ones. To be His "called" ones is to secure the co-operation of all things for our good.[6]
>
> *D. C. Hughes*

AUTHOR'S REFLECTION — God's choice of me is the basis of my view of myself. If the sovereign, majestic God of the universe lovingly and personally called me to Himself, then I am valuable, precious, and loved because of that calling. God paid the ultimate price in adopting me. Not to love Him with my whole heart, and trust Him with my whole life, is to be like an adopted child rebelling against the parents who, at great sacrifice, chose and gave their all for that child.

If I don't truly grasp God's vested interest in me, then it is easy to run or turn away from His discipline and His work to use all things that come into my life for good. It is necessary for me to be reminded that God's perspective on what is good is different from mine. His goal is my conformity to Christ, whereas often my goal is happiness and avoidance of anything that is unpleasant! To rest in God's sovereignty and His ability to cause all things that come into my life to work for good is incredibly freeing. To be assured that the hard, hurtful parts of my life can be interwoven for good keeps me from despair and helps me accept life from the perspective that it all ultimately has meaning. I like what Philip Yancey says: "Faith means believing in advance what will only make sense in reverse."[7]

I do have a choice, though, in how I respond to God's plan for my life. I think of the Israelites in the wilderness. God wanted them to go into Canaan, but they refused. They were still God's children, but they did not experience all that God had planned for them.

It is enough for me to know that God has called me and that He is continually working everything for His good purposes in my life.

> The providence of God so combines with human freedom that, though the ways of God are sure, it is in no sense fatalism. Likewise, the providence of God is the opposite of chance. The divine care reaches to the least detail of life as well as to its greater aspects. Certain attributes of God demand the exercise of His providence. His justice prompts Him to secure all moral good; His benevolence prompts Him to care for His own; His immutability insures that what He has begun He will complete; and His power is sufficient to execute all His desire.[8]
>
> *Lewis Sperry Chafer*

God's Purpose for Me (For Contemplation and Prayer)

8. Over the next few days, think about God's calling of you and His work in you for good. To help your reflection and application, carefully consider the verses below.

> As a prisoner for the Lord, then, I urge you to live a life worthy of the calling you have received. Be completely humble and gentle; be patient, bearing with one another in love.
>
> *Ephesians 4:1-2,* NIV

Use these questions to guide your meditation.

---

9. In what ways do I seek to live a life worthy of God's calling?

---

10. How is God working His good—humility, gentleness, patience, and forbearance—into my life?

SUGGESTED SCRIPTURE MEMORY: Ephesians 4:1-2

CHAPTER SIX

God's purpose:
To Carry Out His Ways
in Our Lives

❦

"For My thoughts are not your thoughts, nor are your ways My ways," declares the LORD. *"For as the heavens are higher than the earth, so are My ways higher than your ways and My thoughts than your thoughts."*

ISAIAH 55:8-9

The beginnings of that transformation which is to change the believing man's nature from the image of sin to the image of God are found in conversion when the man is made a partaker of the divine nature. By regeneration and sanctification, by faith and prayer, by suffering and discipline, by the Word and the Spirit, the work goes on till the dream of God has been realized in the Christian heart. Everything that God does in His ransomed children has as its long-range purpose the final restoration of the divine image in human nature.[1]

A. W. TOZER, *THE ROOT OF THE RIGHTEOUS*

*G*od has a marvelous track record of redeeming impossible situations. He is intent on proving that He is God and there is no other. He delights in receiving glory and He works in surprising ways so that our faith is increased and we are drawn to further dependence upon Him. Gideon had too many men to go into battle; Joshua just needed to shout the wall down in Jericho! Often God's ways seem quite illogical. And sometimes we wonder if He is even involved in what is going on. Certainly His ways are not our ways! But He is sovereign, He has a plan, He loves us, and He has His own ways of working all things together for good.

God's Purpose: To Work His Ways

1. A truth that we can cling to is this: "The way of the LORD is a stronghold to the upright" (Proverbs 10:29). How He works in each of us is unique and different, but He does have some consistent ways of working. Read these Scriptures and write down His way and the expected result.

HIS WAY	THE RESULT
Galatians 5:16-26	
2 Corinthians 4:16-18	

HIS WAY	THE RESULT
2 Timothy 3:16	
Hebrews 12:7-11	

2. What are some of the "ways" of the Lord that have produced good results in your life?

3. It is important to distinguish between God's working the "outside forces" surrounding our lives for good and our own sinful choices that bring His discipline into our lives. These passages exemplify our choices and God's discipline. Write down the choices made and the consequences that followed.

CHOICES	CONSEQUENCES
Miriam and Aaron— Numbers 12:1-15	
Israel— Jeremiah 4:14-18	

God disciplines us with reluctance, though He does it faithfully. He does not delight in our adversities, but He will not spare us that which we need to grow more and more into the likeness of His Son. It is our imperfect spiritual condition that makes discipline necessary. This is not to say that every adversity that occurs in our lives is related to some specific sin we have committed. The issue God is dealing with in our lives is not so much what we *do*, but what we *are*.[2]

Jerry Bridges

God's Purpose: To Have Us Acknowledge Him

4. God's ability to take people's evil intent and work it out for good is exciting, to say the least. God's plans cannot be thwarted even in the face of overwhelming circumstances.

   Read the following passages and record God's use of people's ways to accomplish His purposes.

   Daniel 3:8-30

   Acts 2:22-24

   Philippians 1:12-14

5. Can you recall an example in your life where God worked difficult circumstances for good? Describe your experience.

God called Jesus Christ to what seemed unmitigated disaster. Jesus Christ called His disciples to see Him put to death; He led every one of them to the place where their hearts were broken. Jesus Christ's life was an absolute failure from every standpoint but God's. But what seemed failure from man's standpoint was a tremendous triumph from God's, because God's purpose is never man's purpose. . . . The things that happen do not happen by chance, they happen entirely in the decree of God. God is working out His purposes.[3]

Oswald Chambers

6. God will take events and intervene to accomplish His purpose. But God also will initiate circumstances that will cause us to depend upon Him and acknowledge Him as we never have before. Read these Scriptures and fill in the columns.

GOD'S PART	GOD'S BLESSING
Genesis 22:1-14	Genesis 22:15-18
Job 1:1-12	Job 42:1-17

God is for us far more, at times, than we would prefer. He is committed to removing all vestiges of sin from our soul when we wish He'd be satisfied with a clean new outfit. His interest in us far exceeds our concerns. Our perspective is usually limited to achieving a better life, and His desire for us is radical conformity to His Son's perfect character. No wonder He seems like an enemy when His discipline begins to grind off our arrogance in order to perfect His beauty.[4]

Dan B. Allender

AUTHOR'S REFLECTION—Once while traveling, I took someone else's luggage and she took mine. It wasn't until I arrived at the retreat center, an hour away from the airport, that I realized the mixup. I prayed, "Lord, why did this happen? Now I've got to spend time contacting this person, I'll have to find someone to take a two hour trip, and I need my bag! All of this could have been avoided, this isn't a good use of my time, it's an inconvenience for everyone involved. I don't see any good in this at all!" (I respond well to adversity, don't I?)

This was certainly a very minor irritation in life, but what I learned from it applies to understanding God's ways. As I moved through the next hour arranging this "totally unnecessary interruption" in my life, I began to sense the Lord's thoughts in my heart, "Cynthia, this happened as a reminder that you cannot live life in your own strength or way; more than anything I want you to learn to depend on Me. Sometimes I need to put you into situations, so that you can see Me work and then you will give Me glory. Also, this dear young woman—whose suitcase you have—needs to know of Me, so give her a booklet and write her a personal note."

God's ways are not our ways, but His ways are always right, always for His glory, and always for our good.

God's Purpose for Me (For Contemplation and Prayer)

7. Over the next few days think about how God works and about His desire
   to be acknowledged. To help your reflection and application, carefully
   consider the verses given below.

> O Ephraim, what more have I to do with idols?
> It is I who answer and look after you.
> I am like a luxuriant cypress;
> From Me comes your fruit.
> Whoever is wise, let him understand these things;
> Whoever is discerning, let him know them.
> For the ways of the LORD are right,
> And the righteous will walk in them,
> But transgressors will stumble in them.
>
> *Hosea 14:8-9*

Use these questions to guide your meditation.

8. What is the best response I can have to God's ways in my life?

9. What blessings are mine when I walk in His ways?

SUGGESTED SCRIPTURE MEMORY: Hosea 14:8-9

our purpose:
To Love God and Others

❦

This commandment we have from Him, that the one who loves God should love his brother also.

1 John 4:21

Immeasurable is the effectiveness and attractiveness to others of a pure Christian love; and to the one who thus loves the joyous satisfaction is beyond expression. Little wonder that the Apostle contends that love is supreme and the gift to be desired above all others; nor is it other than proper that love should be named as the first among the elements which comprise the fruit of the Spirit. He who loves with divine compassion drinks the wine of heaven and enters actually by experience into the ecstasy which constitutes the felicity of God.[1]

Lewis Sperry Chafer

To know what God's purpose is in our lives enables us to know what our purpose should be. Because God loves me and wants to conform me to the image of His beloved Son, my life's goal is to "cooperate" with Him, to allow Him to have His way. The highest response to anyone who lavishes redemptive, unconditional love on us is to return that love and please that person in every way possible. And so it is with God. Because of His love, sacrifice, and great care for me, I want to respond to Him and prove my love to Him.

Our Purpose: To Love God

1. How it must grieve God to have to command us to love Him. He is love and we should desire Him and Him alone. Yet because He alone knows our hearts, He must tell us what is best for us. Read these passages and record His instructions.

   Matthew 10:37-39

   Matthew 22:34-38

2. From the above Scriptures, write down your thoughts about the decisions we must make in order to truly love God.

> Have I ever been carried away to do something for God
> not because it was my duty, nor because it was useful,
> nor because there was anything in it at all beyond the
> fact that I love Him?[2]
>
> *Oswald Chambers*

---

3. In order to love God, we must know what He loves. For each of the following passages, record the qualities or actions that please God.

Isaiah 66:1-2

Micah 6:6-8

Hebrews 11:6

Hebrews 13:15-16

4. We know that God wants us to love Him. But God lovingly gives us the choice of demonstrating our love to Him. What do these Scriptures tell us about how God knows that we love Him?

   John 14:19-24

   1 John 5:1-5

5. Take time to evaluate how you express your love for God through obeying His commands. Write down your thoughts.

Do beware of a legal obedience, striving after a life of true obedience under a sense of duty. Ask God to show you the "newness of life" which is needed for a new and full obedience. . . . Believe in the love of God and the grace of our Lord Jesus. Believe in the Spirit given in you, enabling you to love, and so causing you to walk in God's statutes. In the strength of this faith, in the assurance of sufficient grace, made perfect in weakness, enter into God's love and the life of living obedience it works. For it is nothing but the continual presence of Jesus in His love that can fit you for continual obedience. . . . Daily obedience to all that God wills of me is possible, is possible to me. In His strength I yield myself to Him for it.[3]

Andrew Murray

Our Purpose: To Love Others

6. Almost in the same breath with which He asks us to love Him, God also commands us to love others. What can we learn about loving others from these passages?

Matthew 22:39-40

John 13:34-35

1 John 4:7-21

7. Robert H. Benson said, "No man can be a friend of Jesus Christ who is not a friend to his neighbor."[4] Do you agree? Why, or why not?

Give me such love for God and men, as will blot out all hatred and bitterness.[5]

Dietrich Bonhoeffer

AUTHOR'S REFLECTION — As I have gotten older and have been confronted with choosing to do something I know God wants me to do, I am often reduced to one simple prayer: "Lord, if I didn't love you, I wouldn't do this!" Once I was under a time restraint and due to previous scheduling in which I didn't foresee a time problem, I very reluctantly went to speak to a women's fellowship. The meeting was out of town, and I kept telling the Lord that I wished I'd had more discernment or that He had been a "little more" clear about His will for me, for I had prayed about this seminar. This was putting a lot of pressure on me and He certainly knew all I'd be facing at this particular time.

I'm thankful that God honors reluctant obedience. The women at that church blessed and refreshed my spirit. It was just what I needed for that time in my life — to get away, to rest, to be ministered to. (Sounds a lot like the way God works!)

I hate to admit it, but the reason it is hard for me to obey is because it usually means loving people just when it seems most difficult to do so! It involves setting aside my agenda and trusting God to provide the strength, sensitivity, and grace necessary to love. I don't always initially "enjoy" obeying God, but afterward, because of His mercy, I am always blessed.

The psalmist said it beautifully: "How blessed are those who observe His testimonies, who seek Him with all their heart" (Psalm 119:2).

> Mould us, great God, into forms of beauty and useful-
> ness by the wheel of Providence and by the touch of
> Your hand. Fulfil Thine ideal, and conform us to the
> image of Your Son. In Your great house may we stand as
> vessels meet for Your use. We are little better than com-
> mon earthenware, but we may be cleansed, and purified,
> and filled with Your heavenly treasure. Dip us deep into
> the River of Life, and give refreshment by us to many
> parched and weary hearts.[6]
>
> *F. B. Meyer*

My Purpose (For Contemplation and Prayer)

8. Over the next few days, think about how you communicate your love to God and to others. To help your reflection and application, carefully consider the verse that follows.

> My children, love must not be a matter of words or talk;
> it must be genuine, and show itself in action.
>
> *1 John 3:18,* NEB

Use these questions to guide your meditation.

9. How can my love for God be made more genuine?

10. How can my love for others be made more genuine?

SUGGESTED SCRIPTURE MEMORY: 1 John 3:18

CHAPTER EIGHT

our purpose:
TO *W*AIT ON *G*OD WITH *H*OPE

❧

*Since ancient times no one has heard, no ear has
perceived, no eye has seen any God besides you,
who acts on behalf of those who wait for him.*

ISAIAH 64:4, NIV

*If our waiting begins by quieting the activities of
daily life, and being still before God; if we bow and
seek to see God in His universal and almighty oper-
ation; if we yield to Him in the assurance that He
is working and will work in us; if we maintain the
place of humility and stillness, and surrender until
God's Spirit has stirred up in us confidence that
He will perfect His work, our waiting will indeed
become the strength and the joy of the soul.*[1]

ANDREW MURRAY,
THE BELIEVER'S SECRET OF WAITING ON GOD

*I*n our fast-paced, fast-food, "microwave" society, waiting seems entirely out of date and a waste of time. The dictionary gives some interesting definitions for the word *wait*. It comes from the Old English word *to watch*, which according to *Webster's* has these meanings: to stay in place in expectation of; to look forward expectantly; to be ready and available; to remain temporarily neglected or unrealized. Waiting on God and hoping in Him are strong biblical principles and very important in understanding how I am to live my life according to God's ways. If I want His purpose accomplished in my life, then I will learn the discipline of waiting on God and experience the joy that only hope can bring.

Our Purpose: To Learn to Wait on God

1. The psalmists testify to the blessing of waiting on God. Read these passages and write down (1) the benefit of waiting and, where applicable, (2) what the psalmist was waiting for the Lord to do.

   Psalm 25:3-5

   Psalm 33:16-22

   Psalm 40:1-3

   Psalm 62:5-8

2. Paul exhorts the New Testament churches to wait. What do these verses encourage us to wait *for*?

Romans 8:18-25

Philippians 3:12-21

3. How would you explain "waiting on God" to a friend?

To wait on God is entirely and unreservedly to refer ourselves to his wise and holy directions and disposals, and cheerfully to acquiesce in them, and comply with them. The servant that waits on his master, chooseth not his own way, but follows his master step by step. Thus must we wait on God, as those that have no will of our own but what is wholly resolved into his, and must therefore study to accommodate ourselves to his.[2]

Matthew Henry

4. Abraham and Sarah waited many years for their promised heir. Their story exemplifies the blessings of waiting and the consequences of running ahead of God. Read the following Scriptures and record your observations.

a. What was God's promise and Abram's response? (Genesis 15:1-6)

b. What was Sarai's plan? What were the short-term repercussions of their decision? (Genesis 16:1-6)

c. What was God's renewed promise? (Genesis 17:1-8,15-21)

5. Put yourself in Sarah's place and describe what you think she might have learned about waiting on God.

"You'll have descendants as countless as the stars in the sky," God said. No promise could have made Abraham happier. At age seventy-five he still anticipated a tent filled with the sounds of children at play. At eighty-five he worked out a backup plan with a female servant. At ninety-nine the promise seemed downright ludicrous, and when God showed up to confirm it, Abraham laughed in his face. A father at ninety-nine? Sarah in maternity clothes at ninety? They both cackled at the thought.

A laugh of ridicule and also of pain. God had dangled a bright dream of fertility before a barren couple and then sat on his hands and watched as they advanced toward tottery old age. What kind of game was he playing? Whatever did he want?

God wanted faith, the Bible says, and that is the lesson Abraham finally learned. He learned to believe when there was no reason left to believe.[3]

Philip Yancey

Our Purpose: To Hope in God

6. To wait and to hope are closely related. In the Scriptures, "hope" and "wait" are often used interchangeably. Waiting seems to be a measure of our hope. Jeremiah beautifully describes his journey of hope and his understanding of what it is to wait. Read his thoughts in Lamentations 3:1-26 and record your observations.

    a. Describe Jeremiah's hopelessness (see especially verse 18).

b. What was his basis for hope?

c. Why do you think Jeremiah was willing to wait on God?

As believers suffer, they develop steadfastness; that quality deepens their character; and a deepened, tested character results in hope (i.e., confidence) that God will see
them through.[4]

---

7. Read Paul's declaration in Romans 5:1-5 and describe the process that
    leads to hope.

8. Why do you think this process leads to hope?

And hoping is not dreaming. It is not spinning an illusion of fantasy to protect us from our boredom or our pain. It means a confident alert expectation that God will do what he said he will do. It is imagination put in the harness of faith. It is a willingness to let him do it his way and in his time. It is the opposite of making plans that we demand that God put into effect, telling him both how and when to do it. That is not hoping in God but bullying God. "I wait for the LORD, my soul waits, and in his word I hope; my soul waits for the LORD more than watchmen for the morning, more than watchmen for the morning." (Psalm 130:5-6)[5]

Eugene H. Peterson

AUTHOR'S REFLECTION — Many years ago our family made a major move. Jack, my husband, sold his veterinary practice and we relocated to another city to receive training with The Navigators. For years I had been leading Bible studies and now that we had moved to learn to do the ministry full time, I thought that I would probably be leading several studies! As time progressed, I began to realize that God was impressing on me to do nothing concerning ministry. I couldn't understand! Here we had left all that we had known for ten years and now that we were in a position to minister, I was to *wait.* No, Lord, You don't understand — now I'm *supposed* to teach and meet with women!

Yet very clearly and firmly God began to teach me what it means to wait on Him. As Murray says, God wanted me to "maintain the place of humility and stillness, and surrender." What other way could God encourage me and teach me to totally depend on His guidance, His way, His timing? How else could I really learn that my hope was in Him, and not in my abilities?

When the Israelites were in the wilderness, God led them with a cloud by day and a pillar of fire by night. The Israelites did not move until the cloud moved, they *waited* for God to guide.

This waiting is so essential to comprehending God's purpose for us. It is in waiting that we are able to sense God's prompting to do something or just keep on waiting. I like what Oswald Chambers says: "The reality of God's presence is not dependent on any place, but only dependent upon the determination to set the Lord always before us. . . . If our common-sense decisions are not His order, He will press through them and check; then we must be quiet and wait for the direction of His presence."[6]

It is only in being still before Him that we can sense His presence and direction; it is only in placing our hope in Him that we can wait expectantly.

My Purpose (For Contemplation and Prayer)

9. Over the next few days think about how you wait before God and how steadfast your hope is in Him. To help your reflection and application, carefully consider the verse given below.

> Yet those who wait for the LORD
> Will gain new strength;
> They will mount up with wings like eagles,
> They will run and not get tired,
> They will walk and not become weary.
>
> *Isaiah 40:31*

Use these questions to guide your meditation.

---

10. What changes can I make in my life that would encourage my waiting upon the Lord?

---

11. How can waiting for and hoping in the Lord give me new strength?

SUGGESTED SCRIPTURE MEMORY: Isaiah 40:31

our purpose:
TO TRUST GOD
THROUGH SUFFERING

You are given, in this battle, the privilege not merely of believing in Christ but also of suffering for his sake. It is now your turn to take part in that battle you once saw me engaged in, and which, in point of fact, I am still fighting.

PHILIPPIANS 1:29-30, PH

Through affliction He teaches us many precious lessons that otherwise we would never learn. By affliction He shows us our emptiness and weakness, draws us to the throne of grace, purifies our affections, weans us from the world, and makes us long for heaven.[1]

J. C. RYLE

*T*he apostle Peter wrote, "For you have been called for this purpose, since Christ also suffered for you, leaving you an example for you to follow in His steps" (1 Peter 2:21). We have been called to suffer; in fact, Paul writes that it is our privilege to suffer for Christ. Our purpose, our privilege to suffer?—these words seem somewhat strange to our ears today. What is God after? His desire to conform us to the image of Christ and His ways of doing this are certainly opposite of our ways and our thinking. Why must we endure affliction and what should our response be to suffering? Good questions that perhaps can help us begin to grasp God's tremendous heart to have us cling to and live only for that which is the highest, the best, and eternal.

Our Purpose: To Grow Through Suffering

1. We have studied that God works *all* things together for our good. Part of the *all* things is affliction. As you read 2 Corinthians 1:1-11, write down the purposes God has in our suffering.

2. Is there a personal example of suffering you can express? As you look back on your experience, have you been able to discern any of God's purposes that Paul identifies in his letter to the Corinthians? Why, or why not?

Real life requires death. Death involves the experience of suffering. Suffering is required for growth.

> *Even the Son of God was required to suffer in order to enter the fulfillment of His maturity and mission . . . (Hebrews 2:10, 5:8-9).*

Suffering is equally necessary for us because it strips away the pretense that life is reasonable and good, a pretense that keeps us looking in all the wrong places for the satisfaction of our souls.[2]

Dan B. Allender

---

3. Peter's first letter provides a helpful perspective on enduring trials. What truths about God, His purposes in suffering, and our response to suffering can you find in the following passages?

TRUTHS ABOUT GOD	GOD'S PURPOSES IN SUFFERING	OUR RESPONSE TO SUFFERING
1 Peter 1:3-9		
1 Peter 2:18-25		
1 Peter 4:12-19		

4. Describe any struggles you may have with the reality of suffering. Is there a specific Scripture that helps your understanding of suffering?

> Perhaps the most valuable way we profit from adversity is in the deepening of our relationship with God. Through adversity we learn to bow before His sovereignty, to trust His wisdom, and to experience the consolations of His love, until we come to the place where we can say with Job, "My ears had heard of you but now my eyes have seen you" (Job 42:5). We begin to pass from knowing *about* God to knowing God Himself in a personal and intimate way.[3]
>
> *Jerry Bridges*

Our Purpose: To Trust God

5. It is important to remember that when we suffer, we are not alone. Not only is God with us, but our fellow believers share the same experiences of suffering that we go through (see 1 Peter 5:9). Read these verses and record your observations of God's involvement with us in our adversity.

    Psalm 140:12

Isaiah 43:2

Isaiah 63:9

---

6. We are told that we must go through many hardships to enter the kingdom of God (see Acts 14:22). What thoughts are given in these Scriptures that encourage you to persevere in trusting God, increasing your dependence on Him?

Habakkuk 3:17-19

Romans 8:15-18

2 Corinthians 4:7-10

7. What truth about God helps you the most to trust Him? Explain.

Let this encourage those of you who belong to Christ: The storm may be tempestuous, but it is only temporary. The clouds that are presently rolling over your head will pass, and then you will have fair weather, an eternal sunshine of glory. Can you not watch with Christ for one hour?

Bid faith look through the keyhole for the promise and see what God has laid up for those that love Him. You serve a God who keeps covenant for ever. Having already bathed in the fountain of His tender mercies, how can you stand on this side of eternity, afraid to wet your feet with those short-lived sufferings which, like a little splash of water, run between you and glory?[4]

William Gurnall

AUTHOR'S REFLECTION — Several years ago I spoke at a women's retreat. A few years later I was invited back. A dear lady who had been at both retreats came to me and said, "Cynthia, you've grown since you were here before." I thanked her and said that I hoped I was still growing. Later as I thought about her comment and what had happened in the intervening years, I realized that the difference she noticed in my life was the result of suffering.

In the particular trial I had been going through, the Lord seemed to draw a line and ask me if I would trust Him unconditionally. There were to be no promises or guarantees that I would like the outcome. As I pondered the possibility that the struggle I was having might never change or might even get worse, I was crushed. Yet I sensed that the real issue was my choice to cast my burden upon the Lord, trusting that He could take the trial and ultimately work it for His glory and my good.

Oswald Chambers says, "The way to find your self is in the fires of sorrow. . . . If you receive yourself in the fires of sorrow, God will make you nourishment for other people."[5] And so, through our suffering, God is willing to risk His relationship with us so that the relationship can be ever deepened. Whenever we choose to trust Him implicitly, we are freed from the oppressive weight of suffering, we are drawn more intimately to our precious Savior, and other people can see that we have been with Jesus.

> No wound? No scar?
> Yet as the Master shall the servant be,
> And pierced are the feet that follow Me:
> But thine are whole: can he have followed far
> Who has nor wound, nor scar?[6]
>
> *Amy Carmichael*

My Purpose (For Contemplation and Prayer)

8. Over the next few days think about how God uses affliction and suffering to help you grow and trust Him. To help your reflection and application, carefully consider these verses.

> Therefore we do not lose heart, but though our outer man is decaying, yet our inner man is being renewed day by day.
>
> For momentary, light affliction is producing for us an eternal weight of glory far beyond all comparison, while we look not at the things which are seen, but at the things which are not seen; for the things which are

seen are temporal, but the things which are not seen
are eternal.

2 Corinthians 4:16-18

Use these questions to guide your meditation.

_____

9. What encouragements from the Scriptures can help me to persevere
    through suffering?

_____

10. What keeps me from fully trusting God with my life?

SUGGESTED SCRIPTURE MEMORY: 2 Corinthians 4:16-18

CHAPTER TEN

our purpose:
To Serve God with Reverent Fear

Fear the LORD your God and serve him. Hold fast
to him and take your oaths in his name.

DEUTERONOMY 10:20, NIV

We who fear God recognize him as the ultimate
reality, and we respond to him. Fear of God is called
the "beginning of knowledge," meaning that taking
God into account is the foundation of a disciplined
and holy life. To fear God means to reject every
competing deity and to serve him only. Fear of the
Lord is expressed by walking in all his ways, by
loving him, and by serving him with all our heart
and soul.[1]

LAWRENCE O. RICHARDS

*I*t is necessary in our pursuit of wanting to become women of purpose to fully appreciate what it is to fear God. Without the deep respect and reverence one must give to the Lord, it is difficult to really be wholehearted about allowing Him to conform us to the image of His Son. It is also difficult to think about serving God if He is not truly worthy of the sacrifice that serving demands. Peter wrote, "If you address as Father the One who impartially judges according to each one's work, conduct yourselves in *fear* during the time of your stay on earth" (1 Peter 1:17 emphasis added). We are not to be afraid of God, but live in wondrous awe of our heavenly Father and in so doing, we cannot help but want to serve Him obediently with all our heart.

Our Purpose: To Fear God

1. Peter tells us to conduct our lives in reverent fear (see 1 Peter 1:17). Read 1 Peter 1:13-21.

   a. Describe a life lived in reverent fear (verses 13-16).

b. What is the basis for the reverent fear to which Peter calls us (verses 17-21)?

God alone can declare His glory. He is One of whom man should not think without the deepest reverence flooding his heart. God is a terrible Enemy against those who repudiate Him; but to those — even the most sinful — who believe on His Son, He is their God, and all His limitless perfections are engaged in their behalf, and this guarantees that all shall work together for good.[2]

Lewis Sperry Chafer

2. "The LORD favors those who fear Him, those who wait for His lovingkindness" (Psalm 147:11). How do the following Bible characters demonstrate the challenges and blessings of serving the Lord with reverent fear?

a. The Hebrew midwives in Exodus 1:15-21

b. Nehemiah in Nehemiah 5:14-15

c. Peter in Luke 5:4-11

3. Can you identify in any way with these challenges and blessings of fearing God? If so, describe your experience.

> Pay to him humble childlike reverence, walk in his laws, have respect to his will, tremble to offend him, hasten to serve him. Fear not the wrath of men, neither be tempted to sin through the virulence of their threats; fear God and fear nothing else.[3]
>
> *Charles H. Spurgeon*

4. Scripture abounds with the benefits of fearing God. Read these verses and write down the blessings God bestows on those who fear Him. (You might want to add other Scriptures.)

Psalm 25:12-15

Psalm 31:19

Psalm 34:7-9

Our Purpose: To Serve God

5. To serve is to "attend to, minister to, care for, help, be of use, assist, benefit, promote, support, make easy for, nourish, encourage."[4] Paul wrote to the Galatians, "Through love serve one another" (5:13). But as we serve one another, what is our motivation and who are we really serving?

Study these Scriptures and write down your thoughts about where our eyes should be focused and what the attitude of our heart should be.

Psalm 123:1-2

Colossians 3:22-24

The psalm (123) has nothing in it about serving others. It concentrates on being a servant to God. Its position is that if the attitude of servanthood is learned, by attending to God as Lord, then serving others will develop as a very natural way of life. Commands will be heard to be hospitable, to be compassionate, to visit the sick, to help and to heal and carried out with ease and poise.[5]

Eugene H. Peterson

---

6. Oswald Chambers observed that "Jesus Christ calls service what we are to Him, not what we do for Him."[6] Read Luke 10:38-42 and write down your thoughts about how Jesus defines service.

7. As you look at your own life, whom do you identify with more, Mary or Martha? Explain.

Beware of anything that competes with loyalty to Jesus Christ. The greatest competitor of devotion to Jesus is service for Him. . . . The one aim of the call of God is the satisfaction of God, not a call to do something for Him. We are not sent to battle for God, but to be used by God in His battlings. Are we being more devoted to service than to Jesus Christ?[7]

Oswald Chambers

AUTHOR'S REFLECTION — Because I love and respect the Lord, and so want Him to consider me a faithful servant, I want to be confident that what I do, how I serve, pleases Him. As I have thought on the motivation of a true servant and the motivation of one who serves without fearing the Lord, these are my conclusions:

A SERVANT WHO REVERENCES GOD	A SERVANT WHO DOES NOT REVERENCE GOD
Fixes her eyes on her Master.	Fixes her eyes on herself and people.
Is secure because of the consistency of Christ.	Is insecure because of the inconsistency of people.
Serves out of a desire to give.	Serves out of a desire to receive.
Is free to serve, expecting nothing.	Is in bondage to perform, demanding acceptance.
Asks: How can I show Jesus how much I love Him?	Asks: How can I show people how lovable I am?

8. Over the next few days, think about your fear of God and the motivation you have to serve. To help your reflection and application, carefully consider the verses given below.

> Since we receive a kingdom which cannot be shaken, let us show gratitude, by which we may offer to God an acceptable service with reverence and awe; for our God is a consuming fire.
>
> *Hebrews 12:28-29*

Use these questions to guide your meditation.

---

9. How does my fear of God influence my decisions?

---

10. Is my serving from a sincere heart to please God?

SUGGESTED SCRIPTURE MEMORY: Hebrews 12:28-29

my purpose:
To Fulfill God's Purpose

❦

I do not consider myself to have "arrived", spiritually, nor do I consider myself already perfect. But I keep going on, grasping ever more firmly that purpose for which Christ grasped me.

PHILIPPIANS 3:12, PH

The Scotch catechism says that man's chief end is "to glorify God and enjoy Him forever." But we shall then know that these are the same thing. Fully to enjoy is to glorify. In commanding us to glorify Him, God is inviting us to enjoy Him.[1]

C. S. LEWIS, *REFLECTIONS ON THE PSALMS*

The man in the cartoon who walks up to the information booth to ask, "Who am I?" and "Why am I here?" can now be answered. We are beloved children of God, created to be in such vital relationship with Him that we find fulfillment in yielding to His purposes and joy in proclaiming His glory. To live with the assurance that our heavenly Father is personally involved in accomplishing His purpose of conforming us to the image of Christ gives us hope and peace. This perspective on life is not easily explained or understood, but it is God's precious gift to those who deeply love and trust Him and want His purpose above all else.

My Purpose: To Fulfill God's Purpose

1. Deuteronomy 4:9 reminds us, "Only give heed to yourself and keep your soul diligently, so that you do not forget the things which your eyes have seen and they do not depart from your heart all the days of your life." If we truly desire God's purpose, what are some practical ways of "keeping our souls" so that His ways do not depart from our lives? Study these verses and record the ways that will enable us "to keep our souls diligently."

   Psalm 63:1-5

   Proverbs 3:1-12

   Do not yield to the temptation of looking at everything at once, as if everything would happen at once, and all the events of the day be crowded into an hour. Do not thus forecast, but take each thing as it comes to you, and look upon it as the present expression of the will of God concerning you; then regard the rest in the same way, and thus receive your day piece by piece from Him who will remember always when He gives you work to do, that you need strength to do it.[2]

   Priscilla Maurice

2. Jesus told His disciples, "I am the vine, you are the branches; he who abides in Me and I in him, he bears much fruit, for apart from Me you can do nothing" (John 15:5). Abiding in — remaining in, holding fast, continuing in — Christ is foundational to becoming a woman of purpose. What do these verses tell us about how to abide?

   John 8:31

   John 15:10

   Jude 20-21

3. What are some practical ways you can consistently abide in Christ on a daily basis in order to begin to practice those things that will nurture your soul?

> There is only one relationship that matters and that is your personal relationship to a personal Redeemer and Lord. Let everything else go, but maintain that at all costs, and God will fulfill His purpose through your life.[3]
>
> *Oswald Chambers*

4. Just before Jesus ascended into heaven, He instructed His disciples to continue His work on earth. What do these Scriptures tell us about an essential part of fulfilling His purpose?

    Matthew 28:18-20

    Romans 1:16

> There is a glorified Man on the right hand of the Majesty in heaven faithfully representing us there. We are left for a season among men; let us faithfully represent Him here.[4]
>
> *A. W. Tozer*

5. A good summary statement of this study could be that God is always at work in our temporal circumstances to bring about His eternal purposes. Write a brief paragraph stating your understanding of what your purpose in life should be.

6. What does a woman of purpose look like? I think a good description is found in Romans 12:9-21. Read this passage and write down the characteristics of a godly woman who brings glory to God.

"A Puritan Prayer"
O God of the highest heaven,
occupy the throne of my heart,
take full possession and reign supreme,
lay low every rebel lust,
let no vile passion resist Your holy war;
manifest Your mighty power,
and make me Thine forever.
You art worthy to be praised with my every breath,
loved with every faculty of soul,
served with my every act of life.
O help me then to walk worthy of Your love.[5]

AUTHOR'S REFLECTION—I often ask myself the question, "Why do I get up in the morning?" In answering this question, I am reminded daily that my purpose is to get up, set my heart, mind, and soul before the Lord, and walk through the day trusting in His grace and yielding to His plan for my life. This is easy to write, but not easy to do.

I don't like life when I'm hurt, when people won't do what I think they should do, when people I love make wrong decisions, when I'm denied what I think is best. As I look at this last sentence, it is full of "I's." That is the key to understanding *my* purpose—it is not *my* purpose or *my* life—it is *God's* purpose and *God's* life.

I don't want to just "make it" through life trying to grab or manipulate a little peace and happiness as I can. I want the very best that God has to offer while I am here, and I want to offer Him my very best, no matter what my circumstances might be.

I want to stay focused on the things that are eternal: God, Himself, His Word, and people. I want my abiding to grow deeper and deeper so that as others observe my life, they will give glory to God. I want to have the compassion and boldness of Christ in relating to others. This is precious fruit of His Spirit, and it is given only as I abide.

I get up in the morning to become conformed to the image of Christ. What will I give in order for God to accomplish His purpose in me? All that I have and all that I am.

> There is nothing quite as exhilarating as getting out of bed in the morning, going back into the world, and knowing why. Enthusiasm is derived from the certainty that for this I was born, and I am doing it! It is thrilling knowledge that I am fulfilling God's intended purpose for me.[6]
>
> *Bill Hull*

My Purpose (For Contemplation and Prayer)

7. Over the next few days, think about how you are fulfilling God's purpose for your life. To help your reflection and application, carefully consider the verse below.

> However, I consider my life worth nothing to me, if only I may finish the race and complete the task the Lord Jesus has given me — the task of testifying to the gospel of God's grace.
>
> *Acts 20:24, NIV*

Use these questions to guide your meditation.

8. How does my life testify to the gospel of God's grace?

9. How am I fulfilling God's eternal purpose for my life?

SUGGESTED SCRIPTURE MEMORY: Acts 20:24

Are we willing to give ourselves entirely to God; to let Him do with us whatever He pleases; to follow anywhere at His bidding; to renounce anything at His call; asking only, in return, that He will give us Himself, with all His infinite love, to be ours from this time forever? If we are thus willing, let us kneel down at this moment and tell Him so. Alone with God, let us give Him ourselves, all we have and are and shall be, to be unreservedly His.[7]

William R. Huntington

Notes

Chapter One — God's Purpose: A People Who Will Reflect His Glory

1. John Piper, *Desiring God* (Portland, OR: Multnomah, 1986), 43.

2. Lawrence O. Richards, *Expository Dictionary of Bible Words* (Grand Rapids, MI: Zondervan, 1985), 310.

3. J. I. Packer, *Knowing God* (Downers Grove, IL: InterVarsity, 1973), 155.

4. Piper, 228.

5. A. W. Tozer, *Men Who Met God* (Camp Hill, PA: Christian Publications, 1986), 23, 25.

Chapter Two — God's Purpose: To Conform Us to Christ

1. David Brainerd, quoted in *Giant Steps*, Warren W. Wiersbe, ed. (Grand Rapids, MI: Baker, 1981), 64.

2. Charles H. Spurgeon, *Morning and Evening* (McLean, VA: MacDonald Publishing Co., n.d.), 24 December.

3. Oswald Chambers, *My Utmost for His Highest* (Westwood, NJ: Barbour and Company, 1935), 23 July.

4. Lewis Sperry Chafer, *Systematic Theology* (Dallas, TX: Dallas Seminary Press, 1948), 195-196.

5. Chambers, updated version (1963), 22 July.

Chapter Three — God's Purpose: To Love His People

1. C. S. Lewis, *The Four Loves* (New York: Harcourt Brace Jovanovich, 1988), 126-127.

2. Philip Yancey, *Disappointment with God* (Grand Rapids, MI: Zondervan, 1988), 209.

3. Yancey, 115.

4. Dan B. Allender, *Bold Love* (Colorado Springs, CO: NavPress, 1992), 83.

5. Lawrence O. Richards, *Expository Dictionary of Bible Words* (Grand Rapids, MI: Zondervan, 1985), 421.

Chapter Four — God's Purpose: To Establish His Kingdom

1. A. W. Tozer, *The Knowledge of the Holy* (San Francisco, CA: Harper & Row, 1961), 119.

2. Jonathan Edwards, quoted from John Piper, *Desiring God* (Portland, OR: Multnomah, 1986), 22.

3. James Boice, quoted by Charles R. Swindoll, *Growing Deep* (Portland, OR: Multnomah, 1986), 99.

4. Lewis Sperry Chafer, *Systematic Theology* (Dallas, TX: Dallas Seminary Press, 1948), vol. 2, 75.

5. Philip Yancey, *Disappointment with God* (Grand Rapids, MI: Zondervan, 1988), 91.

6. C. Donald Cole, *Thirsting for God* (Westchester, IL: Crossway, 1986), 188.

Chapter Five — God's Purpose: To Accomplish His Plan for Good

1. Oswald Chambers, *My Utmost for His Highest* (Westwood, NJ: Barbour and Company, 1935), 30 August.

2. Lewis Sperry Chafer, *Systematic Theology* (Dallas, TX: Dallas Seminary Press, 1948), vol. 3, 167.

3. Lawrence O. Richards, *Expository Dictionary of Bible Words* (Grand Rapids, MI: Zondervan, 1985), 316.

4. Chambers, 25 July.

5. Jerry Bridges, *Trusting God* (Colorado Springs, CO: NavPress, 1988), 151.

6. D. C. Hughes, quoted in *The Biblical Illustrator*, Joseph S. Excell, ed. (Grand Rapids, MI: Baker Book House, 23-volume edition), vol. 17, 177.

7. Philip Yancey, *Disappointment with God* (Grand Rapids, MI: Zondervan, 1988), 201.

8. Chafer, vol. 1, 256.

Chapter Six — God's Purpose: To Carry Out His Ways in Our Lives

1. A. W. Tozer, *The Root of the Righteous* (Harrisburg, PA: Christian Publications, Inc., 1955), 60.

2. Jerry Bridges, *Trusting God* (Colorado Springs, CO: NavPress, 1988), 150-151.

3. Oswald Chambers, *My Utmost for His Highest* (Westwood, NJ: Barbour and Company, 1935), 5 August.

4. Dan B. Allender, *Bold Love* (Colorado Springs, CO: NavPress, 1992), 118.

Chapter Seven — Our Purpose: To Love God and Others

1. Lewis Sperry Chafer, *Systematic Theology* (Dallas, TX: Dallas Seminary Press, 1948), vol. 6, 206.

2. Oswald Chambers, *My Utmost for His Highest* (Westwood, NJ: Barbour and Company, 1935), 21 February.

3. Andrew Murray, *The Treasury of Andrew Murray* (Grand Rapids, MI: Baker, 1969), 157-158.

4. Robert H. Benson, quoted in *The New Book of Christian Quotations*, compiled by Tony Castle (New York, NY: Crossroad, 1989), 152.

5. Dietrich Bonhoeffer, quoted in *The New Book of Christian Quotations*, compiled by Tony Castle (New York: Crossroad, 1989), 151.

6. F. B. Meyer, quoted in *Joy and Strength*, Mary Wilder Tileston, ed. (Minneapolis, MN: World Wide Publications, 1988), 92.

Chapter Eight — Our Purpose: To Wait on God with Hope

1. Andrew Murray, *The Believer's Secret of Waiting on God* (Minneapolis, MN: Bethany, 1986), 21.

2. Condensed from Matthew Henry, on "Communion with God," Charles H. Spurgeon, *The Treasury of David*, vol. 1 (McLean, VA: MacDonald, n.d.), 401.

3. Philip Yancey, *Disappointment with God* (Grand Rapids, MI: Zondervan, 1988), 66.

4. *The Bible Knowledge Commentary*, John F. Walvoord and Roy B. Zuck, ed. (Wheaton, IL: Victor, 1983), 456.

5. Eugene H. Peterson, *A Long Obedience in the Same Direction* (Downers Grove, IL: InterVarsity, 1980), 140.

6. Oswald Chambers, *My Utmost for His Highest* (Westwood, NJ: Barbour and Company, 1935), 20 July.

Chapter Nine — Our Purpose: To Trust God Through Suffering

1. J. C. Ryle, quoted in *Closer Walk* (Walk Thru the Bible Ministries, Inc.), 8 November 1990.

2. Dan B. Allender, *The Wounded Heart: Hope for Adult Victims of Childhood Sexual Abuse* (Colorado Springs, CO: NavPress, 1990), 180.

3. Jerry Bridges, *Trusting God* (Colorado Springs, CO: NavPress, 1988), 190.

4. William Gurnall, *The Christian in Complete Armour*, revised and abridged, vol. 1 (Carlisle, PA: Banner of Truth Trust, 1986), 163-164.

5. Oswald Chambers, *My Utmost for His Highest* (Westwood, NJ: Barbour and Company, 1935), 25 June.

6. Amy Carmichael, *Thou Givest . . . They Gather* (Fort Washington, PA: Christian Literature Crusade, 1958), 90.

Chapter Ten — Our Purpose: To Serve God with Reverent Fear

1. Lawrence O. Richards, *Expository Dictionary of Bible Words* (Grand Rapids, MI: Zondervan, 1985), 272.

2. Lewis Sperry Chafer, *Systematic Theology* (Dallas, TX: Dallas Seminary Press, 1948), vol. 1, 224.

3. Charles H. Spurgeon, *The Treasury of David*, vol. 1 (McLean, VA: MacDonald, n.d.), 124.

4. J. I. Rodale, *The Synonym Finder* (Emmaus, PA: Warner Books Edition, 1978), 1093.

5. Eugene H. Peterson, *A Long Obedience in the Same Direction* (Downers Grove, IL: InterVarsity, 1980), 62.

6. Oswald Chambers, *My Utmost for His Highest* (Westwood, NJ: Barbour and Company, 1935), 19 June.

7. Chambers, 19 January.

Chapter Eleven — My Purpose: To Fulfill God's Purpose

1. C. S. Lewis, *Reflections on the Psalms* (San Diego, CA: Harcourt Brace Jovanovich, 1958), 96-97.

2. Priscilla Maurice, quoted in *Joy and Strength*, Mary Wilder Tileston, ed. (Minneapolis, MN: World Wide Publications, 1988), 98.

3. Oswald Chambers, *My Utmost for His Highest* (Westwood, NJ: Barbour and Company, 1935), 30 November.

4. A. W. Tozer, *The Knowledge of the Holy* (New York: Harper & Row, 1961), 124.

5. "A Puritan Prayer," in *Decision Magazine* (April 1989), 40.

6. Bill Hull, *Jesus Christ Disciple-Maker* (Colorado Springs, CO: NavPress, 1984, out of print), 71.

7. William R. Huntington, quoted in *Joy and Strength*, 31 July, 213.

AUTHOR

Cynthia Hall Heald is a native Texan. She and her husband, Jack, a veterinarian by profession, are on full-time staff with The Navigators in Tucson, Arizona. They have four children: Melinda, Daryl, Shelly, and Michael.

Cynthia graduated from the University of Texas with a BA in English. She speaks frequently to church women's groups and at seminars and retreats.

Cynthia is also the author of the NavPress Bible studies *Becoming a Woman of Excellence*, *Becoming a Woman of Freedom*, *Becoming a Woman of Prayer*, *Intimacy with God*, and *Loving Your Husband* (companion study to *Loving Your Wife* by Jack and Cynthia), and *Becoming a Woman Who Walks with God*.

BECOME A WOMAN OF GOD

Becoming a Woman of Freedom

If you feel like your Christian life is weighing you down, this Bible study will give you a second wind and help you identify and lay aside those burdens that make you feel "stuck."
Cynthia Heald   1576838293

Becoming a Woman of Prayer

God designed women to seek Him in all they do. This Bible study will encourage you to become a woman whose life is characterized by constant conversation with God.
Cynthia Heald   1576838307

Becoming a Woman of Excellence

This best-selling Bible study has helped over one million women understand who God designed them to be. Discover the freedom you have to serve and please God.
Cynthia Heald   1576838323

"DEEP IN MY HEART IS THE CONSTANT PRAYER THAT I WOULD BE A WOMAN WHO CONSISTENTLY WALKS WITH GOD."
–Cynthia Heald–

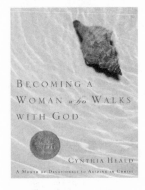

Becoming a Woman Who Walks with God
1-57683-733-5

Essential to walking with God is maintaining communion with Him. This devotional book, designed to guide you through a month of quiet times, emphasizes the joy and the importance of abiding in Christ.

Each of the thirty-one daily meditations in this collection includes a Scripture passage, insights from the author, a thought-provoking quote from a classic Christian writer or thinker, a question to ponder during the day, and a short topical prayer.

Join Cynthia on a journey of reflection and worship, and discover the joy of becoming a woman who walks with God.

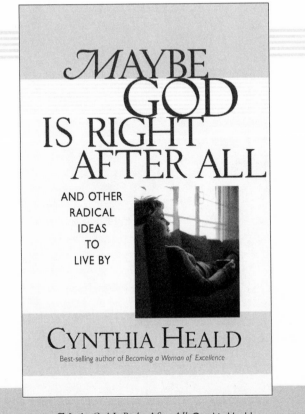

MAYBE GOD IS RIGHT AFTER ALL

AND OTHER RADICAL IDEAS TO LIVE BY

CYNTHIA HEALD

Best-selling author of *Becoming a Woman of Excellence*

In *Maybe God Is Right After All,* Cynthia Heald offers ten bottom-line truths, tested and proven in her own journey, to equip readers to make godly choices at the crossroads of their own life circumstances.

Softcover
ISBN 1-4143-0084-0

Release date:
OCTOBER 2005

TYNDALE